ACHILLES' MEMOIRS

ACHILLES' MEMOIRS

by

H. N. Levitt

Mellen Poetry Press
Lewiston•Queenston•Lampeter

Library of Congress Cataloging-in-Publication Data

Levitt, H. N.
    Achilles' memoirs / by H.N. Levitt.
        p. cm.
    ISBN 0-7734-3084-9 (paper)
    1. Achilles (Greek mythology)--Poetry.   2. Trojan War--Poetry.
I. Title.
PS3562.E92225A64   1998
811' .54--dc21   98-36307
                                                                      CIP

The Edwin Mellen Press   The Edwin Mellen Press
Box 450   Box 67
Lewiston, New York   Queenston, Ontario
USA 14092-0450   CANADA L0S 1L0

The Edwin Mellen Press, Ltd.
Lampeter, Ceredigion, Wales
UNITED KINGDOM SA48 8LT

Printed in the United States of America

To Terrin

PREFACE

Achilles has been a favorite of poets since Homer told us he was willing to lose a war because he wanted the woman his commander-in-chief had taken from him. And Homer, in his no-nonsense way, describes the events that led to Achilles finally getting his girl, going out and defeating the Trojan hero Hector, and getting things rolling toward victory—a victory he would not survive.

These memoirs are not really memoirs as we think of them. Achilles couldn't write. It's rather as though the great hero—actually little more than a teen-ager—were speaking to you, the reader, directly. Think of it that way when you read this poem.

Homer would never put up with such wallowing. But we in the late twentieth century are wallowers. We love to get inside people's heads. And so did I. I imagined a scenario that appears neither in Homer nor anywhere else in the Greek myths, but nevertheless, is the way that I chose to see the intimate details of Achilles' story. I hope it will please you.

This is the story
of a jealous man
who stopped at nothing.

I put this story down in writing more
for myself than for others, for these
are things I can only say to myself,
to understand the conflicting feelings
I've not been able to shake off.

I'm not one for words. Words
faze me for they have many meanings
but what I feel now is as clear as a brook
falling on the same smooth stones forever.
I feel anger, anger with myself.

This is the story of the lies that thrive
in women for they are the ones who
make men war against themselves and
each man within himself. Men
cannot win wars brought by women.

Patroclos is gone, Hector is gone,
Even Briseis stolen then grudgingly returned
by brute Agamemnon is gone.
Only the savagery of the campaign,
the deaths and sacrifices remain.

In due time I'll complete the rout
of the Trojans and I'll flush
Paris and deal him the same fate
of his brothers Troilus and Hector,
for though I may be angry with myself
there'll never be an end to my temper.

When the king took goldenhaired Briseis
from me I cursed the day I was born.
I swore in silence at his duplicity
for he had always had his eye on her.
Squaring the score was his excuse to take her.

I walked straight away kicking the sand
pounding my fists against the boat.
I mounted Pedasus and dashed away
flashing toward the walls of Troy.
I would have killed every Trojan alive

for the hate I had for Agamemnon, but I
desisted, calmed by Patroclos who followed me
and I returned, my cousin by my side,
and we gave Briseis over to the lust
of the most selfish Achaean of the host.

In the short time we were together,
beautiful Briseis, my gentle cousin Patroclos,
and myself, I suffered a dream that was
so real pity I didn't take it so,
for then the truth would have led me

to understanding, and that to the quiet
in my spirit that defends me. I dreamt
in the brittle cold of dawn I was struck
from behind hard to the foot, though my greave
came fully round from the shin and knee.

I went crashing down defenceless
awaiting the end, yet I couldn't see
my enemy for the clouds of dust swirling
over me. But then there was a settling
and what I saw pierced my heart like a knife.

Patroclos and Briseis held a spear that
they thrust again as one, but I turned in time
and with all my strength I rose up
and confronted them. They fell to their knees
pleading for mercy. I beheaded them in one blow.

3

I awoke in a hot sweat, and Patroclos,
who always lay by my side, shook me
gently to banish the horror of that sleep.
On my other side lay Briseis curled
in the crook of my arm smiling in blissful sleep.

I was utterly confused and for some moments
I forgot who and where I was. To have
kindness and beauty awaken me from
that nightmare quite distracted me
from my senses and I was helpless.

Thinking of it now my fury rises
at that picture of blissful innocence on the face
of the sleeping Briseis, the look of innocence
as often the wayward mask of deceit
as it is the faithful expression of goodness.

But at the time I was so pleased with her
that I sent Patroclos away so that Briseis and I
could be together away from intruders.
I was so infatuated with her loveliness
that I insisted even Patroclos

be alien to this love, even he become
no more than a Myrmidon like the others
to be kept at a distance, in their place.
Briseis gently held me in her arms
and I must have felt something of love.

I did all, I killed Troilus for her
and begged her father on my knees
to let me carry her from the Trojan camp.
I told her mother I see in all directions
but her girl of mirrors is always in my eyes.

They drove me away to cool my heels
to walk off passion on the battlefield
but so desperately did I want their girl,
though they never understood it,
no one would stop me from taking her for myself.

I returned, brushed Calchas aside,
and with my armorplated right arm
swept her up by her slender waist
and carried her through the fighting mob
all of them parting before my terror.

Women against men. There's the story
of the war for Troy. For me at the very outset
it was the cruel king Agamemnon slaughtering
his daughter at Aulis, that sweet girl
I loved from the distance of my boyhood.

Before that the war began when the whore Helen
sacrificed all for love that
lasted no longer than a second sigh
in Paris's ear, and he the fool
playing on that sigh the music of the deaths

of the great heroes of the cities of the Aegaean,
all for her, men destroyed and Troy ruined.
Polyxena was another one, casually striding
the walls of Troy sucking on grapes and
defying the blood, dust, and carnage below,

upsetting us with her beauty so cleverly
that I humiliated myself pleading with Priam
were I to have her I'd give him my full cache
of Trojan spoils: gold, bronze, horses, armor,
purple cloaks, silver tripods, all but Briseis.

Priam laughed. "What madman of a father
would give his favorite girl to an enemy?"
he said. So I told him outright, then and there,
she'll be mine even though she lay
in the grave with me, she will be mine.

Unfaithful Penelope in Ithaca, still another one,
they say she fouled her husband's bed
long before he undertook the expedition
and it's said even now thin-legged,
barrel-chested Odysseus fights by my side

blind to his dishonor all these years since.
Clytemnestra, there's the one. She and I
share the knowledge of Agamemnon's
double nature: the gift of lying
through his teeth, and the need for women.

He's the one who decapitates his child
as he anticipates feasting on the women of Troy
and when he doesn't get his way nothing
short of murder answers his disappointment.
His wife knew it first and I'm told she plays

two faces to his one. She'll have it out.
Perhaps it isn't so much the women as the men
who prime them into deeds only war disposes.
Perhaps it isn't the women at all
though I find myself unconvinced of that.

Such distractions take me from my story.
How I go on! The one who wasn't one for words!
I fought the enemy for Briseis, and I fought
my own treacherous king for her, and when
she became mine my eyes were always on her.

My eyes were on Patroclos as well
as long as I remember him beside me
and always so in the house of Peleus
where I spent my boyhood far away
from my divine mother always distant

from me. Patroclos I loved the most
for he was kind and gentle and held me
on his sturdy shoulder and protected me
as he would himself— no, even more
did he watch over my life than his own.

These two, then, these two did I love
as only one can love beauty and kindness
and they, in turn, cherished and honored me
and each other as well. They were
as joyous as I in each other's presence.

Do you know what it's like for three
loving friends to share each other?
There's always someone left waiting,
you might say, that nothing is perfect,
but it would be the expected mortal view,

those unaware of the immortality of it.
No. Each loving gesture is threefold
and each threefold yes is never forgotten.
It is a strength of its own kind
away from battle or a part of it.

Enough to say they were my own two
and I revelled in them as a child
revels in his older brother and sister
for they were both older than I. I led
my Myrmidons to Troy when I was fifteen.

Others were children at that age but I
had already conquered the skills and tactics
of war and not one Greek or Trojan
alive doubts, today and then,
I am the greatest and noblest of all,

I, Achilles, son of the goddess Thetis,
no man is swifter or stronger than I.
But there is no peace in my heart, then what good
is great strength and fleetness of foot if a man
cannot sleep and when awake he trusts no one?

He cannot live with himself nor with others,
silence is his enemy and his deeds become chaos
before his eyes. He makes no sense of existing
and spends hours in distressful contemplation
on death and the favor of no longer being.

What is it that brought me to this state
of despair? A few chance words cried out,
themselves in despair, but they were words
like stones falling on my helmet, each one
heavier than the last, adding to the pain.

When the king took Briseis from me I brooded
many months. I refused to fight and kept
my Myrmidons idle or performing time-
consuming tasks or competing half-heartedly
at funeral games for the allies killed.

One day Patroclos stood before my tent
in anger, his arms akimbo and his legs
bestride the sand like a colossus.
"Our best men, and Agamemnon, Diomedes, Odysseus
are either wounded, dying, or dead, and here

"you sit nursing lovesick wounds over a girl
because the king took her from you. You brood
while the allies go down to defeat. Are you
the same Achilles I love? I say
you're not, you've lost your courage!"

He who that same night lay beside me
in friendship and trust stood before me now
accusing me of cowardice, me Achilles!
I lunged to my feet and stood him full face,
towering over him now where once

he towered over me. In fury I grasped
his neck and would have strangled him
had he fought me, but he stood his ground
seemingly content to have me kill him,
so the fury spent, I clasped him to me.

"Patroclos, dear cousin, how can you
have become so angry with me since
last night when anger was the last thing
in either of us? What have I done
so recently to deserve this outrage?"

"It's what you haven't done," he said.
"Just your presence on that field in your
shining armor would put such fear
into their hearts the Trojans would panic
and run like deer at the sight of a lion."

"I decided and I stand by my decision,"
I told him. "Until that Briseis is returned
to me—he knows she is mine alone!—
no amount of entreaty, even from you,
will convince me to fight for that whoremaster!"

"Then I'll use other strategy," he said,
turning away the flap of the tent
and gently escorting beautiful Briseis
before me. "The king's guards who favor you
let her come to see you for a single hour.

"Maybe she can convince you of the
folly of your decision." And with that
Patroclos stepped outside to guard the tent.
Here she was then, the cause of all
the dissension, lovely as ever, and so close

I could reach out and touch her golden
hair, but we both stood silently searching
each other's eyes, I so shy I lost my tongue,
and her face formed into a gentle smile
at my discomfort as she led me to the rug.

"How can you be the one to convince me
to join the war that I quit for not having you?
What happens when you're with the beast king?"
I was beset with doubts, with suspicions
of Agamemnon, of course, but also of her.

As though I had never spoken she smiled
as before and caressed my face with her hand.
Then breaking silence she said that such things
did not belong in this tent. Whatever Greeks
and Trojans do or don't is their affair

but love is far more precious than war
and whether I fought or not meant nothing
to a slave. She had never referred to
or thought herself a slave with me.
I considered what changes had come over her.

"Then why are you here, Briseis," I asked her,
"if war is not your argument what do you
and Patroclos intend with this secret visit?"
"I'm here to tell you you are my master
and I'll never love anyone but you.

"And you should consider Agamemnon
with all his bluster will never have me.
If you take the field do it for the Greek cause
and to set my mother and father free
and then I swear I'll be yours forever."

14

She kissed me gently and placed my hand on her breast,
but I called in Patroclos and had him
take her back to the brute in his ship,
and I pondered long into the night
on the state of affairs and what I must do.

And by the first rosy streak of dawn
I had decided clearly how I would proceed.
I walked out among my ships, greeting
the sentinels and chiding the ones who slept
by their posts, my voice alone waking my men

whom I gathered strong about me, my sturdy
warriors filling the beach from the water's edge
to the bluffs leading to the field of battle.
"My men! I have orders for you!
Do your tasks at once! We will fight!"

At that, they gave forth a great roar
that must have been heard beyond the walls
of Troy, and they must have shaken with fear
for they know as all the world knows,
nothing can stop my brave Myrmidons!

Then I called in Patroclos dearheart
and I had him sit in comfort on the rug.
His face brightened at the prospect
of going into action, but he was
still ignorant of my intentions.

"My men are entering the war," I said,
"and leading them into battle astride Pedasus
will be my shining armor, the fearful black
horsehair plume above my great helmet
will shake fear into their Trojan hearts

"and they'll be cut down like stalks of wheat,
like frightened horses they'll run
every which way to avoid their deaths.
We will be the ones to clear the field
to the Trojan walls which will then be breached!"

"How happy I am you have come to your senses!"
he said. "It was beneath you to stake so much
on a girl. Honor and victory are the issues
that occupy great generals, and Achilles
in my eyes is the greatest general of all.

"Nothing can stop you once you put your mind
to it—neither Hector nor Paris nor any lesser
Trojan in the field who always take to their heels
when they see the sun flashing on your armor
like a blazing fire, your sword cutting their men

"to pieces, putting Trojans to death in droves."
I looked deep into his eyes for the truth
but I found nothing convincing there.
The eyes of Patroclos were as unyielding
as they had been from the first.

"Listen closely to me, Patroclos," I said.
"Pedasus will be there and my armor will
be there with you in it. You, second to me
alone in all the Greek legions, you
will lead our forces to victory.

"Let Trojans think they face me. The armor alone
will drive them helter-skelter over the field
and you'll pick them off like flies.
You'll do honor to me, and on your return
the Greeks will learn it was you triumphant!"

He was aghast. He shook his head trying
to reach an understanding and he said
nothing. He merely looked into my eyes
expecting more, but face to face I was silent.
I could see Patroclos was bewildered,

joy and despair warring in his soul.
"You yourself came to me angry," I said.
"You said I had lost my courage. A mere girl
had me nursing lovesick wounds. I say
you may be right, my courage may have flown

"as the spirit leaves the body knowing
there is no longer a home for it.
Achilles without courage is defenceless
but if there were one to act in my place
who but you, my cousin, would he be?"

"Whatever you say is mine to accept," he said,
"and I can see the ingenious scheme in it,
so you have my unqualified yes
and the eagerness already in my bones
to get on with it and take the field,

"but I don't understand why
Achilles would not want to assert himself
since the girl is easily won over.
I hope you know my anger was my enemy
when I foolishly questioned your courage."

I stared into his eyes. It was some time
before I spoke. "No mortal is capable
of defying me," I told him. "My mother
is always near and when she seeks it
she has the attention of almighty god.

"Should I allow a mere Agamemnon
to control my destiny? It's crucial
that I have my way, that any man
suffer the cruelties of the gods
if he dare dictate conditions to me.

"There are no conditions that guide my fate.
My mother and the immortals decide that.
When Agamemnon comes to me on his knees
and places Briseis on my ship with all
the gifts befitting me, then, and only then

"will I consider winning the war for him."
This did I say, and though it was audacious
to declare such vanity, these were
my feelings, and I could not control
their expression in the face of his doubts.

But Patroclos took up the challenge
and bravely galloped to the field
in my flashing armor and bestride
my godlike horse Pedasus, the two
of them leading the army of Myrmidons.

I had my tent moved to an unseen spot.
Two sentinels and I were all that remained
of the Myrmidon host at the edge of the sea.
And though I heard the mayhem in the distance,
the battle joined by my mighty forces

I retired to my tent more than ever
dark, questioning, disquieted in my heart.
I did not know if I had done right
by the two I loved, brave Patroclos
and that enigmatic girl, brighteyed Briseis.

But what troubled me more was the thought
of love itself. How could I love someone?
Whom could I trust? Early and deep
were my first feelings of loss
when Iphigeneia perished before my eyes.

I knew then despising Agamemnon
would be an unrelenting passion.
That sweet girl was most like myself,
courageous, unafraid of the future
and gifted with the spirit of life.

But I was too young to save her, too shy
to stand against her intemperate father.
I let him destroy that lovely girl
in the name of this misguided mission
to bring a whore back to her cuckold.

It troubles me. Something is wrong.
It should never have come to this, Patroclos
taking my place on the field even though
only he is second to myself
and none among them is equal to him.

I continue to worry about these things.
How would I know if I had really
lost my courage. Do I know myself
enough to know that? There were many times
when fear, like some thundering monster,

stormed behind me, his black cloak spread
to take me in and force me off the field
in shame, the times I doubted
my invincibility, all that blather
of immortality, being merely a man.

I don't really know what it is I want,
treating Briseis with suspicion, and sending
my loving cousin away like that.
Why am I alive if my own mother,
benevolent Thetis, measures the string

of my time? It's wrong to know our death
for how can we then live peacefully?
I am young, yet my time
has been in warfare, arrogantly.
I blame women for men's distractions,

for the joy men have in killing each other,
the ecstasy of it, wallowing in blood,
gore and dust. What has all that to do
with women who end up slaves amid
the vagaries of victories and defeats?

I am not at peace with myself.
Away from the action is a terrible
place to be, turning inwardly,
falling on doubts and questions
pressing in the back of one's mind.

There was a sudden silence in the distance
where the din of battle had consoled
me in my dread thoughts.
Now there was dread in the silence.
I sent one of my two men to see,

but before he could leave there stood
Antilochos, having dismounted, in tears.
"Patroclos is dead. They have even killed
the great horse Pedasus, and to make
matters worse, Hector took your armor!"

I sent him away. I sent my sentinels away.
There were distractions I could not
share with others. They know nothing
of the signs of grief in someone like me.
They know nothing of my ways.

There are times when my heart grows cold
so quick I fear it will never warm again.
I sent Patroclos to his death
though of all men only he
was the one I wanted by my side.

But I would not show them my grief,
and the Achaeans said never had they
witnessed such deep, quiet mourning
in a warrior as lofty as myself,
and they wanted me all the more to fight.

The savaged corpse of Patroclos was brought
to me by Odysseus who carried him
in his arms though he was sorely wounded
himself. I preferred to be alone and
took Patroclos in my arms into my tent.

For a long while I stared into
his opened eyes, opened by Death—
ever the trickster when he takes us—
and I could hear Patroclos
calmly speaking to me from the grave.

"Did we love or did we hate each other?"
he said. "I was most kind to you, Achilles,
but where was your kindness to me?
How did you dignify me? You mistrusted me.
Now isn't that the truth of it?"

The corpse was all questions. "Dignity
was in my being," I said. "Eternity
was what I gave you. Your death
is the first hint of my own. Shall we
weep like women over our endings?"

Suddenly his eyes closed. It was Death
capable of being alive, once again
tricking us. And tricked I was.
I had never answered his questions.
Did I exalt my cousin Patroclos?

Never. Never. I am my own glory.
I am proud. It was only
my unfortunate nature, kin of Thetis,
that dictated my inability
to feel human compassion,

being led by a divine mother
and an all too human father,
both of whom managed in their
devious ways to pull me one way
or the other to their philosophies.

Patroclos. I washed the mud and gore
from his face with water and scented oil
and it was as though the touch of his skin
brought me to the depths of the quandary
that had been working in me.

I knew he would die when I sent him
on that hopeless mission because armor,
however ominous cannot shield a lie.
Greatness reveals itself in actions.
It can never be replaced by parody.

His death is part of my string of time.
We're all done away one way or another
in this senseless war. Even the living
are never the same, none of us, none of us
survive without some mortal wound.

The death of Patroclos made them attend me.
More than ever before the Agamemnons
pleaded with me while tending their wounds
to save them from their certain defeat.
But still I held out. They couldn't reach me.

It isn't enough for Patroclos to have loved me.
He should have honored me. How often
does an immortal live among them?
He said I had lost my courage.
A thwack of a sword is nothing to an insult.

The Agamemnons came to my tent,
Ajax, Odysseus, the whole string of them,
to show me they shared my mourning
and to beg without shame for me
to take up the cause in their desperation.

I agreed immediately. I'd have
Briseis returned and all manner of spoils
to accompany her. Agamemnon
assured me, taking me aside,
that she was intact as far as his intent.

So the exchange was made. I dispatched all
and I stood in the shadows waiting.
When Briseis was brought into the tent
she was faced with the becalmed hero Patroclos
who was scented and dressed for her grief.

Immediately she fell upon him
caressing his face and weeping
bitter tears, clutching and wailing
and keening like a forlorn child,
tearing her hair at the sight of his mangled body.

"Oh, my beloved!" she cried. "Once again
I lose the only one dearest to my heart!
First my brothers, then my husband by the spear
of Achilles, and now you, forced to take
his place on the battlefield and in death!"

When she saw me she threw herself
into my arms and wept all the more
for the loss she meant to share with me.
Even in tearful grief she was the image
of golden Aphrodite born from Chaos.

No man could not be moved
by such heart-rending sorrow in one
so clearly meant to be adored.
Merely by placing my arm gently
on her shoulder I welcomed her

back and despite her display of grief
I told her I would build a temple of love
to honor immortal Aphrodite in her name,
and the time would be coming soon
when her losses would be revenged.

What is one to make of things said
in passion or grief or in distraction?
Where does the truth lie—in what is said
or in what is done? Is there
a weakness we all share in not knowing

deep, deep in our hearts what it is
we really are, what it is we
should know ourselves to be? Can we
be that blind that we think ourselves
good when we are the faults, the blemishes?

I know the deception in myself.
I don't imagine I am different
from others. We're all deceivers.
What truth would I die for?
The way is to get through as best

one can, for all of life is like this war.
It weaves back and forth, from one
side to the other. Who can say
if the victor is the one who wins?
He himself knows it was all by chance.

Men live or die mostly by accident.
Briseis putting the death of Patroclos on me
changes entire ways of seeing and thinking
though I mean not to punish her
for the grief she lays on me.

All deceit is eventually known
because the thing is what it is
whether feigned by women or men.
It can't disguise itself indefinitely;
the truth is forever undermining

its purpose: to say and to appear
to be the opposite of what one is
to the end of finding safety.
Well, the world is not safe. Kings
are taken into slavery and live

their entire lives in penury away
from friends and family, given up
to the whims and demands of tyrants.
If this can happen to kings
how can others expect to escape?

Briseis imagines her beauty
can save her from harsh Fate
all must be prepared for.
But beauty only survives
when stress is not its sister.

31

I'm not to forget these memoirs
are meant to enlighten me, being
more for myself than for others. Briseis
is a distraction from the dilemma
of the pitiable death of Patroclos.

I am uncertain but he may
have died because I wanted him to,
and he may have known that I sent
him to his end despite my claims
of love and concern, the urging of care

that accompanied the send-off.
Then it may be that I hate Patroclos,
he, of all, whom I professed to love,
as I would have it against anyone who for
whatever reason longed to take my place.

But he succeeded. He took my place with her.
And when he led my Myrmidons
I know something quickened in his heart.
"But for a quirk of Fate this bright armor
would have launched me to heroism

just as glorious as that of Achilles,"
he must have said to himself. How
could he have avoided the temptation?
He surely must have said that,
otherwise what horror is there for me?

I'm still young, in my twenties now
and I'm not expected to be
all-seeing. There isn't much expected
of me in wisdom of any sort
because I'm young, I'm impulsive.

I believe I don't really understand
what it is for people to love each other.
Should we expect anything more?
Should I hate Briseis because in my heart
I know she is indifferent to me?

One is torn by these dilemmas
because they put off doing
and there are crucial things to do
far more important than
wasting time thinking about love.

How is it possible to explain
why I want her more than before
though I know she plays me
against her eventual freedom
giving me good reason to ruin her?

These memoirs put to me questions
for which there are no answers
under the Sun. Let this thing
spin out to its conclusion. Let
darkness sweep its cover over us

in preparation for the light of day
and the demand the Sun makes on men
to go about it seeking their ends,
the work of Greeks and Trojans alike
on this blooded, trampled field of war.

I place the Briseis near me but
far enough away that I can recognize
the slightest discomfort in the look
on her face, so intent am I
to capture her real meaning.

"It seems we both loved Patroclos," I said,
"as though there were no other human being
as deserving. I am moved
by your heartfelt grief at the
sight of our hero so mangled and torn."

"A grief we both share," she said,
"for he was the most gentle warrior
and the most amiable of men."
Far from being diverted her eyes
were fixed on mine intently.

"Why are you so challenging?" I said.
"There's danger for you in this
attitude. In a fit of temper,
so typical of me, I could
cut you from your life at once."

"There never was a time when I didn't
know that," she said, "so I have
learned to live with the threat. The truth
is that love and hate like day and night
endlessly follow each other."

Some think the past is only time gone by
but I know from my mother that we
cannot avoid the past; it's forever
renewing itself in remembrances
that hinder the present like ghosts

that take on form and substance
and must be reckoned with before we can
go on. In such a way do the ghosts
of Troilus and Diomedes hover
over the destiny of bold Briseis,

the girl in cunning far beyond her years
who speaks like the sage or the contriver
depending on the direction of the wind.
This Briseis who held back victory
by the challenge of her beauty, she rests

languidly on the rug before me
imagining that nothing in her words
or her behavior offers the slightest threat
to her life. She sees herself as
innocence on a monument, glorified.

This is the girl who loves as the spirit
moves her. She loved her husband Mynes
whom I killed in the field like the others.
But far from mourning him she spied Troilus,
the spoiled son of Priam, and there was hope

and expectation in her. Effeminate
as he was Briseis saw no distinction
between love pursued and love gained
and so she became Troilus' darling
during the time she spent in Troy.

As was to be expected, when I
killed Troilus, merely another Trojan son,
and Briseis was taken by me as spoils
and then stolen by brute Agamemnon,
what misery did she inflict on herself?

She spotted Diomedes among the Achaeans,
the bravest and most lordly warrior
of the Argive host, and though she offered
herself to him and he was taken with her
they say he held off in deference to me.

That may be so or it may not.
A shadow of doubt always touches her.
One can never be certain that
what is said is what had been done or
what is not said had not been done

because a woman desperate to gain
advantages will say or do anything,
so it seems to me, shy as I am
of experience in these things. Briseis
is one to be loved but not trusted.

"I can see by the changes in your face,"
she suddenly said, "that all kinds of dire
consequences are in it for me.
The little boy Achilles is once again
out for vengeance for things either done

"or imagined done. Why should I,
who have lived with all this death,
fear death of my own? I tell you,
Achilles, nothing you say or do
has the power to intimidate me."

"You are mine. I took you fair and square
which is the way of war. It's honorable
for spoils to be given and agreements made;
it's the civilized way of waging war.
I don't intimidate what is mine

"but I have every right to demand love
if my courage makes me deserve it.
You're meant to love me; it's your duty,"
I said straight to her, but she smiled
that familiar, devious smile,

leaving it to me to form my own
conclusions. "Because of you," I said,
"men die needlessly. The least you can do
is love me, as I have every right to expect.
Stop exchanging men at every whim

"of Fate. When I take to the field the war
will soon be over. Patroclos said I will
take you for my wife. He was right,
but only because I had told him so.
You must love me. It's what I request."

I had my say and I believed I had
expressed my feelings very well. There
was no need to shilly-shally about it
any longer. But the Briseis girl
stared at me and remained silent.

When the silence began to grate on my nerves
she spoke. "Love is not possession," she said,
"it's contemplation. It's not a thing
that can be made done. It's something
that comes from outside in, by itself.

"It cannot be declared for this or that
reason. It can only . . . " but I
interrupted her. "Briseis, you can't
forever hold off the inevitable.
How can a woman not love Achilles?"

"Aphrodite will tell you," she answered.
"Fame, glory, and reputation
hold no power over her because she
goes straight to the heart of us humans
and she enjoys defying expectations."

I could not understand her meaning.
I told her I'd promise never
to hurt her, never to use my strength
as an advantage, and to regard
other women only as friends or strangers,

never in intimacy or in the thought of it,
although if the truth be told, and I
have vowed to do so in these memoirs,
as advanced as I am in warfare
I am far less experienced in love,

as Briseis well knows, but the ingenuity
that scored my progress in fighting
will easily be put to the same service
in making me more capable in love,
and so she would be well advised,

even at this late stage, to learn
to love me if only for her own good.
She took my hand. It was a pleasantry,
one of few ever coming from her.
I waited for words but again there were none.

"I'll be your friend, as was Patroclos,"
she said, "but I'll never caress or dally
with you—though I have trifled at times,
I admit—but that was for the purpose
of encouraging your good graces

"to continue to protect me. As for love,
you're far too young for me, Achilles.
I prefer men of more mature years.
I don't mean to hurt you, Achilles,
but as you said, 'the truth is the truth.' "

Is it possible to imagine such audacity
face to my face? There was a trembling
in me that I knew as that temper
that in the past had led me to such
extremes of violence that I slaughtered

enemies without knowing who they were,
and without caring. I'd kill whoever came
into the curve of my broad sword,
and there were times, horrible times,
when my own allies fell by my fury.

But I'm strong in many ways, and now
I summoned strength to curb my wrath,
to give the girl every chance to pause
and reconsider words that were rash
but surely not given from the heart.

"That is the way things are," she said,
"and I can well imagine the pain inflicted
on your pride, but it has nothing to do
with that. You are still glorious, Achilles,
but not the same way in my eyes."

"Initiate me, Briseis. Let me
learn how to love with your help
and I will understand and accept
your preference, which is, after all,
what I'd expect from a woman

"of your experience. I'm too much
taken with myself to appreciate
the truth is not always what I want.
Show me what Aphrodite means
by the joy of defying expectations."

Briseis laughed, but in a way that
wasn't meant to humiliate me.
"Most women would love to initiate
a warrior hero into the sweetness
of love. And so would I. I yearn

to be your best, if only for the
pleasure and privilege. What is it like
to take on an immortal? I shiver
in expectation, Achilles. Do what
you will. Like Pedasus, mount me!"

I led my instincts with her guidance
and I witnessed what mortal men
consider the highest ecstasy of all.
I must be true to myself if these memoirs
are to have any belief in them.

What I shared with Briseis was enjoyment
of a kind, but what needs to be done
far exceeds Aphrodite's enigma.
Who knows? It may be those of us
with immortal blood in various ways

respond differently to the high
passions so frenzied about
among the others. It may be
Aphrodite is a snare to turn
men's heads away from Necessity.

I tried not to prolong the pain.
I hit Briseis with the flat side
of my broad sword and she was
gone in an instant. The movement
from life to death was imperceptible.

I turned away and strove to consider
the things I should do to confront Troy,
but before that I thought it fitting
to express some tribute to the
spirit of this most beautiful of girls.

It's not in my nature to feel remorse
because immortals do what must be done
impersonally, and though one may question
my immortality, as I confess,
I do, myself, still, I have their blood.

It was destined, Briseis, that you be
put aside. There was far too much
fuss made over you, mostly by myself,
of course. But the worst mistake of all
was that you imagined you could treat me

as you would other men. You couldn't see
that I'm not one of you, I'm beyond
human, and though your ears are deaf
to revelation I'll speak to your spirit.
Aphrodite's game has no interest for me.

Then I can see you in a light
none other can. I can see your life
deep in distress for all the men gone
that choice or circumstance visited
on you. I also see you cared for none

of them, myself included, as you
so boldly said. You suffered
the disadvantage of being a woman.
Pity you couldn't see how much
I understand the common flaw

that men imagine they're superior
in ways merely for their maleness.
In truth, sex is a disadvantage
because it gives one an excess of only
half of what is needed for excellence.

The best humans are those with both
qualities, and in that sense I am
eminently eligible, being
the issue of a god-given union:
a powerful goddess and the bravest of men.

You were a noble princess but sooner or later
you would have been put away
because a woman without a preference
is not to be trusted and is predicted
to turn on almost anyone, and

no one can be secure with her
because nothing is worth her keeping.
Without preference humans are in chaos
and life and even war exist to impose
order so that the strongest survive

with cause, or at least with control.
You created chaos among the Greeks
because too many of us wanted you,
and since your preferences were tentative
you were doomed from the start.

You should have wanted me, Briseis,
because the world wants me; no one
has ever turned his back on Achilles.
You put too much store in what
you call your feelings and how

unfortunately they did not include me.
Feelings are devious and figments
of imagination often contrary
to one's best interests. Live by feelings
and you don't live long in this world,

which, of course, you discovered all
too soon. But you should have preferred
me as so many others do, because I
clearly and dangerously made you
my preference, almost to the downfall

of the Greek cause, and where has it
ever been written that an immortal
could be dispensed with impunity?
My mother told me early that
though I'm among you I'm not of you.

All of them but you knew that.
So you're gone with your lover beyond
the dark river. I'm left to contemplate
my deeds, given they exist remorseless;
these were the ways you were both to go.

"But why, mother, are you so certain,
speaking to me now?" her usual voice
just over my shoulder, although she
a world away winging on silver feet.
"You always keep me away from sorrow

"as though I were not man enough
to deal with it. You taught me well
but if I could see you once that would be
more than all the lessons, all the words.
I long to see your astonishing beauty."

49

And for the first time in my life

I was shown a vision of my mother,

the goddess who saved Zeus from death,

goddess of the sea-deeps, and she

who burned my brothers save only myself,

who made me swift of foot like herself.

When I left for Troy she gave me my father's armor

and the great ash spear and sent me off

with gold and silver and her lips to my brow,

the softness which I felt but could not see.

"I named you Achilles because you had placed

no lips to my breast," she said, "and so

I place my lips on you, dear child,

to repay my short-sightedness."

I'll not forget. That was what she said.

Now she appeared before me in brilliant

thin silver armor like the scales

of a fish, her golden hair falling

below her irridescent helmet of the same

silver, a sturdy silver trident in one hand.

"This is the fourth month of the year, my darling,"
she said, "the time for you to take up arms."
But by now I had become entangled
in my offenses. I had thought too long
of them and they had taken my mind.

"You know what I have done," I said to her.
"Deliberately I put my friends away.
How can I fight with a clear conscience?"
"Conscience," she said, "has no meaning
to those like us who are timeless

"and far beyond them, whom we only touch
in passing time to time. They are
like anchors who drag to the bottom
anyone they can in their desperate
attempts to keep from falling to the depths,

"but fall they must, the matter is when,
nothing more. They dream too much
and they seek their dreams in reality,
which is the most pathetic exercise
conducted by these pathetic humans.

51

"Conscience is fear and we cannot afford
such luxury. Do everything
dispassionately because what you do
is always what had to be done
so that the balance is kept between

"those who live and those who give
them life. Now, to you, my sweet son.
The Armorer himself has made a stunning
coat, leg braces, and helmet for you,
and War-lover Ares has given you his spear.

"You will take to the field with the sun
blazing on your armor. You will look
like fire mounted on your steed Bay
and all within reach will go down
before you. You'll be invincible."

But then, suddenly, it was as though
a cloud had passed over her lovely face,
and she turned away from me to hide
tears. "Tell me what it is, mother,"
I said. "Tell me what I already know."

"My dear child," she said, "the world
will soon lose you; even I will never
again see you. Though you will be
glorious, and all of them, allies and enemy,
will be dauntless, you will not survive.

"You will be thrown down to the dust,
your beauty and your glory spoiled.
It is fated to be your last battle.
There will be one, far less deserving,
who will put an end to your life."

I could not avoid the irony
of Patroclos, Briseis, and I dying
within a few days of each other.
He who kills is killed himself in turn
whether or not he be immortal.

It all comes to the same thing: endings.
What is begun in such high spirits
ends always in ruined expectations.
We live. We die. We cause great suffering
along the way. Then, it's over, over forever.

I dared not touch my mother, but I
tried to show her with my eyes on hers
that I understood. I would fight
fiercely to the end, keeping this memory
of her beautiful vision in my mind.

(The memoirs end here. On the next day Paris, the
weakling, who stole men's wives, stood on the Trojan
wall from a long distance and pierced Achilles with a
lucky arrow shot to the heel. So began Achilles'
terrible end.   He suffered days and nights of
continuous pain until he was finally relieved by Death.)

About the Author

H. N. Levitt is a retired professor of drama and theatre history at Hunter College in Manhattan. Before that, he was an assistant editor of *The American Poet*, a post World War II small poetry magazine that managed to publish many outstanding American and European poets.

He also writes plays and has had four full-scale Off-Broadway productions. One play, *One Foot to the Sea*, ran two-and-a-half years at The Actor's Playhouse in Greenwich Village and received the Best Play of The Year award from *Off-Broadway* magazine.

He's the co-founder of The Poetry Society of Woodstock whose year-round monthly Saturday sessions at Town Hall have featured many outstanding poets, not merely regional ones. Individual poems of his have appeared in various places, but he particularly likes having had *Art Times*, a cultural publication dedicated to the arts, publish *The Oracles of Soho*, his second favorite book-length poem.

H. N. Levitt
Photo by Mary Ann Zotto